Nannie Doss — The Giggling Granny

A True Crime Story of America's
Female Serial Killer, Her Poisonings,
Victims, and Chilling Confessions

Richard B. Wray

1

DISCLAIMER

This book is based on **verified historical facts**, official case files, court transcripts, interviews, newspapers, and documented sources about Nannie Doss.

It is written **in a narrative, documentary-format** to enhance readability, but **all events, timelines, and outcomes reflect factual information available in public records**.
 No scenes, dialogue, or descriptions are intended to misrepresent real individuals or fabricate unverified claims.

This book does **not** glorify violence or crime.
 It aims to inform, educate, and provide historical context about a real criminal case and its impact on society.

Reader discretion is advised due to descriptions of crime and sensitive subject matter.

DEDICATION

To every reader who seeks truth in the shadows,
 and to those who believe stories—especially dark
ones—
 can teach us more about human nature than we ever
expect.

And to the families affected by real cases everywhere:
 Your courage and voices matter.

ACKNOWLEDGMENT

I would like to thank the historians, archivists, librarians, and true crime researchers whose work preserves cases like this for future study.
Your dedication to factual accuracy makes books like this possible.

To the true crime community—authors, podcasters, documentarians, and investigative journalists—thank you for continuing to ask difficult questions.

And to my readers:
 Thank you for choosing this book and allowing me to guide you through one of America's most unsettling cases.

Contents

AUTHOR'S NOTE

This book is told in a **storytelling narrative**, but every
detail is rooted in **verified facts, documented timelines,
historical interviews, and court records**.
 My goal is to present the case in a way that feels
immersive and emotionally gripping, while maintaining
full respect for the truth and for the real lives impacted
by Nannie Doss's actions.

I believe true crime should do more than recount events.
 It should help us understand the psychology, the societal
failures, and the warning signs we often miss.

Thank you for reading, and for stepping into this story
with an open mind and a desire to learn.

Prologue

The Smile That Hid a Killer

The laughter was the first thing everybody noticed. It drifted through the modest cottage in Blue Mountain, Alabama, a lilting, pleasant song that could make even the most nervous neighbor grin. Nannie Doss glided across the room with a deliberate lightness, pouring sweet tea to visiting relatives, her eyes gleaming with warmth. On the surface, she was the perfect grandmother, the welcoming face of household joy. Children clung to her skirts, neighbors communicated their concerns over the fence, and acquaintances praised her as constantly compassionate, attentive, and fascinating.

But beneath that appeal, a keen observer may have spotted the smallest spark of calculating. Nannie's grins were occasionally too timed, too purposeful. A buddy recalls her hands lingering over her husband's shoulder a second too long before a taste of dinner was offered. In subsequent years, investigators would look back on these small, innocuous-seeming instances and see them as part of a pattern, early indicators of a deceptive mind deliberately learning to navigate the environment.

Her childhood gives clues that were never clear at the time. Born in 1905, Nannie grew up in a household that mingled warmth with neglect, affection with inconsistency. Family stories depict her as vibrant and naughty, quick to captivate adults, quick to rebel when frustrated. Teachers praised her brilliance and wit, but also a streak of intransigence and a tendency to manipulate peers to get what she desired. These qualities, harmless in early youth, would later grow into tools of control and deception.

Long before her neighbors would speak about strange illnesses or deaths, the first victims were already in her orbit. Family members who died abruptly, husbands who grew ill without evident cause—each episode was a whisper of what was to come. In 1933, her first husband, Charley Braggs, died after only a brief period of marriage. To outsiders, it was sadness, the sort of abrupt disaster that could strike anyone. Only later would the pattern emerge: the stream of husbands, lovers, and relatives whose deaths were discreetly mysterious, always leaving Nannie unharmed and socially intact.

At gatherings, she laughed, recounted stories, and offered comfort. Her presence looked pleasant, even comforting. Yet every interaction, every carefully provided meal or prescription, was part of a concealed dance. When neighbors reported her cheerfulness, investigators years later would reflect on how successfully she concealed darker urges behind household routine. The very traits that made her beloved also made her deadly—a paradox that would define her legacy.

By the time the first traces of her misdeeds were pieced together, it was nearly unbelievable. How could a lady so commonplace, so seemingly innocuous, be responsible for the murders of eleven people—and probably more? It was a question that would torment law enforcement, the media, and the public alike. Nannie Doss had mastered the art of invisibility, her fatal intent masked by laughter, charm, and the carefully maintained image of the perfect grandmother.

The whispering began lightly, nearly inaudible, like a draft beneath the door. But as the years progressed, and as detectives traced the lines from one inexplicable death to another, it became clear: behind the warmth and happiness, a darker story was waiting to surface. The grin that had welcomed neighbors, children, and relatives alike was the same smile that hid a life of deliberate murder.

And in that knowledge, the first terrible fact became undeniable—sometimes evil does not announce itself with screaming. Sometimes it giggles.

Chapter 1

Childhood Shadows

The house in Blue Mountain, Alabama, was modest and worn, its white paint cracked in spots, the wooden steps groaning with every footfall. Inside, the air smelled faintly of soap, bread, and the tang of ancient wood. Nannie Doss was born in 1905 into a world that seemed commonplace on the surface but had undercurrents that would subtly influence her. Family members described a home filled with both affection and stress, a place where warmth coexisted with unpredictability.

"Nannie was always lively, always getting into something," her relative would recount years later. "She had a spark in her eyes, like she knew something the rest of us didn't."

Her parents, George and Emma Doss, were described as affectionate yet inconsistent. George worked long hours on the farm, a quiet man of few words, while Emma's attention swung between doting and stern reprimands. In this setting, Nannie learnt early that charm might gain her favor. She would flirt with the grownups in the room, provide courteous smiles, and twist a simple anecdote into laughter that would linger.

School was another arena where her personality took shape. Teachers described her as intelligent, fast with responses, and socially adept—but with a touch of cunning. She could persuade the teacher into overlooking misconduct, or convince students to give her what she desired. "She was smart, too smart sometimes," one teacher recalled. "You could see she liked being in control, even as a little girl."

But alongside this intelligence came solitude. Nannie was not always invited to play by other youngsters. She was observant and conscious of exclusion, learning to observe rather than participate at times. Her brilliance allowed her to navigate social situations with ease, although she remained an outsider in subtle ways. Family friends later described her as "sweet, but always a little apart, always watching."

And then there were the instances that hinted to something darker. Stories from her teenage years emphasize pranks that crossed limits, tiny acts of brutality that went unrecognized or were regarded as mischievousness. She had a preoccupation with the fragility of life, a curiosity that seemed benign until analyzed retrospectively. There were tales of her testing the effects of alcohol on family or experimenting with minor dosages of substances, though these occurrences were never completely documented at the time.

At home, her interactions with her mother and father often mingled affection with manipulation. "Nannie could make you laugh, and then make you feel guilty at the same time," Emma Doss reportedly recalled in a family reminiscence. Her charm was a tool, even in youth, to bend things to her advantage. Conversations generally ended with Nannie smiling sweetly while gently transferring blame or focus.

The loss of her grandparents and the diseases of close relatives left subtle imprints on Nannie. Children of her era were expected to confront mortality more directly, and she learned to see emotions to grief and dread. Neighbors would observe years later on how young Nannie seemed unusually unshaken by tragedy. She would attend wakes and funerals, her face calm, her eyes interested, as if collecting the behaviors of others rather than grieving in the traditional manner.

Her first marriage at age 19 to Charley Braggs, though years removed from her first fatal deed, had roots in this early societal training. She had grown accustomed to using charm to navigate relationships, a talent that would eventually benefit her in far darker ways. Even as a child, Nannie appeared to realize that the world responded to appearances, to the smile on her face rather than the motives behind it.

"Do you think she knew what she wanted from the start?" a distant cousin would question decades later. "I think she was just... learning the rules. How to make people trust you, how to bend them without their noticing."

The strands of her childhood—charm, cunning, curiosity, and detachment—interwove to build a foundation that would silently support a life of manipulation and murder. There were no overt warnings, no unambiguous indicators, only a sequence of behaviors, patterns, and observations that, seen in hindsight, constituted a horrifying blueprint.

By the time Nannie reached maturity, she had perfected the art of perception. She may appear pleasant, attentive, and innocent, while simultaneously calculating, observing, and judging how to attain her aims. The seeds placed in Blue Mountain, fostered through charm and wit, would eventually develop into something that startled a nation—a lady capable of killing lives while remaining a revered grandmother figure.

And yet, even in those early years, there were whispers, little moments of uneasiness that few could define. A sudden harshness in her tone, a momentary glance at a sibling, a covert smile when something unpleasant occurred. These shards, seemingly trivial at the time, would later be combined in the imaginations of investigators and criminologists to reveal the growing contours of the Giggling Granny—the woman who could disguise fatal intent beneath laughter, tenderness, and the carefully maintained impression of normalcy.

Chapter 2

The Many Marriages

Nannie Doss's adult life was marked by a series of marriages, each one seemingly ordinary, each one quietly ending in tragedy. To the casual spectator, she was lucky in love, a caring wife, and subsequently, a delightful grandmother. But behind closed doors, a pattern of deception and murder was slowly forming, disguised beneath her continuous grin.

Her first marriage to Charley Braggs lasted barely a little period before his death. To the neighbors, it was heartbreak, the kind that haunts little towns abruptly and without explanation. Nannie was inconsolable—or so it appeared. Family tales remember her sitting silently at the kitchen table, wiping tears, while taking detailed records on daily chores. "She cried," a cousin would remember decades later, "but it was the kind of crying that made you think she knew something we didn't."

By the time she married her second husband, Charlie Harrington, the pattern of her life began to cement. She moved from state to state, cultivating a persona of gentleness and attentiveness, while carefully testing the waters of each new connection. Friends and neighbors were attracted by her laughing, the way she carried herself, her ability to turn every simple domestic moment into love and comfort.

"I never would have guessed," one neighbor told detectives years later. "She baked cookies for the whole block, sang in church, and smiled at everyone… and yet…" Her sentence trailed off, the unspoken mistrust lingering in the air.

For each husband, Nannie tried subtle methods. She studied habits, listened for weaknesses, and prepared her environment. Arsenic became her tool of choice—a gradual, almost imperceptible means to control life and death. She would add small amounts to food or drink, always just enough to make a death appear natural, leaving no instant suspicion.

Her third marriage, to Arlie Lanning, followed the same pattern. She moved into his home, learnt his routines, and made herself indispensible. In the kitchen, she would converse casually while stirring coffee, testing the reactions, evaluating the tolerance, her humor hiding calculating. "She was the sweetest person you could imagine," Lanning's neighbor later remarked. "She never missed a chance to help, but she had this... look, sometimes. Like she was always thinking two steps ahead."

Nannie's husbands have described her as attentive, affectionate, even playful. They could not perceive the underlying manipulation, the way she carefully regulated their life, their food, and eventually, their health. "I thought she loved me," one spouse revealed in later interviews. "I thought she was my companion... but looking back, there were warning signs I ignored."

Despite the disasters that followed her, the public impression of Nannie remained overwhelmingly positive. Church organizations, social gatherings, and neighbors all complimented on her warmth and humor. She appeared to be the ideal wife, mother, and later grandmother—a woman who could create joy out of the mundane. That exact normalcy became her cloak, allowing her to continue her atrocities across decades and states without raising suspicion.

Even in the aftermath of each husband's death, Nannie would return to usual activities with astonishing ease. She attended funerals, comforted mourning friends, and smiled at family gatherings, all while investigators would eventually reveal her deliberate manipulation of events behind the scenes. Every meal cooked, every act of concern, was calculated.

In private moments, however, Nannie's thoughts were elsewhere. Investigators' notes from later interrogations indicate her reflections: the satisfaction in managing life and death, the thrill in watching her schemes succeed without notice. She would observe her next potential husband quietly, noting habits, rituals, vulnerabilities. Every relationship becomes an experiment, every domestic environment a testing ground.

By the time she married Richard L. Morton, her eleventh husband, the pattern was clear. Investigators piecing together the decades of deaths noticed the deliberate accuracy, the recurrent use of poison, and the amazing regularity of circumstances surrounding each dying. Yet at the time, she remained invisible to the public view, the pleasant, charming woman who baked cookies, shared laughing, and attended church services without a trace of suspicion.

"Do you ever think she felt guilty? " one cousin asked years later. "I don't think she did. She was... cautious, calculated. Always cheery, always nice. That was her armor."

And so, the succession of weddings continued—a trail of spouses, lovers, and residential spaces subtly molded by a lady whose outward attractiveness disguised lethal intent. Each union ended in heartache, illness, or death, leaving behind bereaved families and communities stunned by the sudden loss.

The next husband, wherever he arrived in her life, would be just another chapter in a pattern. Nannie's grin remained steady, her laughing light, and the world around her naive. But in her own meditations, she was already planning, calculating, monitoring, waiting. The cycle would recur, leaving investigators years later to track a string of disasters that no one could have believed were linked—and a lady whose sheer normalcy was her worst weapon.

Chapter 3

The Giggling Granny Emerges

The sound that everyone recalled most was the chuckle.

It wasn't loud. It wasn't forced. It was a sweet, fluttering giggle—almost girlish, unusually delicate for a lady who had lived through several marriages, terrible relationships, and the grinding weight of rural poverty. That chuckle wafted across kitchens, front porches, and church socials. It followed Nannie Doss like perfume.

And it disarmed everyone.

Neighbors in North Carolina, Alabama, and Kansas alike remembered her as nice, helpful, cheerful. A woman who baked pies, held newborns, and told humorous anecdotes about her husbands' idiosyncrasies. "Lord, that woman could laugh through anything," one neighbor would later declare in a recorded interview. "Happiest person you'd ever meet."

But by then, of course, the truth had already surfaced.

Years previously, they had no cause to suspect anything at all.

Nannie sat on a porch swing in Lexington, swaying softly while putting sugar into a glass of tea. The afternoon light sliced through the slats of the wooden porch, turning her face warm and gentle. She giggled as she informed her sister about her newest "silly magazine romance."

"They promise so much in those letters," she murmured, stroking a lock of hair. "A woman can't help but laugh at the foolishness of men."

Her sister chuckled, oblivious of the emerging trend behind Nannie's marital history.

At the time, the neighborhood saw only the version of Nannie she wanted them to see—the friendly woman who worked in the house, kept gardens, reared children, and smiled through adversities. No one looked too hard at the catastrophes that seemed to follow her: husbands dying unexpectedly, children falling ill, relatives passing away suddenly. In the 1940s and early 1950s, disease was rampant, life expectancy uncertain. Early deaths were rarely questioned.

Nannie leaned into that.

In one interview transcript decades later, a neighbor recalled a particular occasion when Nannie's husband, Samuel Doss, grew gravely ill.

"She sat right there in the waiting room," the woman remembered, "just gigglin' and chattin' with me about sewing patterns. Didn't appear worried at all. I questioned her, 'You sure you're okay? And she answered, 'Well, Sammy's powerful. He'll be just fine.' Then she laughed—light, like a girl laughin' at a joke."

The neighbor paused in the interview, shaking her head.

"I should've known something was off. But back then... you trusted folks. And Nannie? She was the last person you'd suspect."

In numerous towns she resided in, people described the same contradiction: Nannie had charm that didn't match her surroundings. She was a woman who had experienced many marriages, several abusive relationships, financial instability, and immeasurable personal loss. Yet she presented herself as cheery, upbeat, almost comical.

At church functions, she brought casseroles and peach cobblers. At community functions, she offered entertaining stories. At home, she clipped love-magazine advertising, grinning as she circled attractive bachelors.

"She could make you feel like she'd known you forever," a former neighbor recounted. "She'd grab your hands, look right in your eyes, and say, 'Honey, everything's gonna be alright.' And you believed her. That's the kind of woman she was."

But behind closed doors, her facade started to break.

One evening in 1953, a family friend named Ruth stopped by unexpectedly to offer extra vegetables from her garden. She knocked quietly and glanced inside.

What she witnessed wasn't dramatic—just a fleeting moment. But later, it would loop in her memory like a scene trapped in slow motion.

Nannie was standing at the stove, stirring something in a pot. Nothing strange. But her expression—just for a second—was blank, distant, almost frigid. Like someone entirely isolated from the world around her.

Then she heard Ruth.

"Oh honey! I didn't hear you come in! " Nannie chirped. And the giggle returned instantaneously, like someone switching a light switch.

Ruth later told police, "I brushed it off at the time. Everybody feels fatigued now and then. But the way her smile popped back on… it wasn't normal."

Moments like those were small, short, but undeniable. The giggle always returned. The warmth always reappeared. And thus the uncertainties faded.

When relatives began dying one after another, people searched for explanations—but not at Nannie. They blamed ill luck, food poisoning, the infirmities of old age. When two of her children died in early childhood, family members mourned without ever challenging her. When her grandson died suddenly, again no one looked her way.

Doctors filled up death certificates. Communities sent condolences. Nannie prepared more casseroles and carried herself with serenity that everyone mistook for strength.

"She was the strong one," a cousin claimed years later. "We leaned on her. And all that time…" The cousin's voice broke. "All that time, she was the one we should've feared."

But the first suspicions didn't come from family. They came from someone who didn't know her history—someone who regarded her not as a sweet grandma but as a new bride who hovered a little too enthusiastically near her husband's meals and medicine.

In early 1954, Samuel Doss's doctor would recall how bizarrely Nannie acted while Samuel recovered from a mysterious sickness. When Samuel regained strength and decided to return home, the doctor told him bluntly:

"Don't let anyone prepare your meals for a few days."

Samuel bowed politely, not realizing the weight of the warning.

Days later, he was dead.

And with his death, for the first time, a doctor took up the phone and phoned the police.

The world that once perceived Nannie as a harmless granny will soon discover that the giggle wasn't innocent.

It was camouflage.

Her laughter, her charm, her flawless Southern hospitality—they were all part of a mask disguising the reality. And as investigators prepared to inspect Samuel's body, the cracks in that mask widened for the first time.

The community's blind trust was about to clash with the chilling truth of a woman whose smile had covered years of death.

And for the first time, someone was finally staring straight at her.

The next chapter would uncover the first official suspicions—and the first indisputable evidence that broke the façade forever.

Chapter 4

The Poisoner's Toolkit

The sound of a spoon tapping gently against a glass established a familiar beat in Nannie's kitchens. A slow, steady clink… clink… clink… followed by a quiet giggle flowing through the room.

For years, the tiny routine remained unnoticed.

It wasn't sinister at first glance—just a grandmother pouring tea, or coffee, or a pot of stew boiling on the stove. The ingredients were always ordinary. Sugar. Milk. A pinch of nutmeg. Sometimes homemade jams are folded into biscuits.

But detectives would eventually uncover that Nannie's kitchens contained another ingredient—one that didn't belong in any recipe.

Arsenic.

More specifically, arsenic-laced rat poison, commonly available across Southern general stores during the 1930s, 40s, and early 50s. Cheap. Reliable. Nearly undetectable in remote settings with minimal toxicological resources. And when incorporated into food or drink? It tasted like nothing at all.

Perfect for a woman who built her life around a charming smile and a disarming chuckle.

Investigators would later reconstruct what they suspected happened inside Samuel Doss's home in 1954, using interviews, medical reports, and Nannie's own ultimate confession.
Samuel loved coffee in the evening—something simple to wind down before reading his books. He drank gently, appreciating tranquility after a long day of work at the warehouse.

Nannie knew this.

She also knew that arsenic dissolved rapidly in warm liquid.

In a dramatic reenactment decades later, Captain Bob Bristow, who worked the case, recalled the scenario with clinical calm:

"She'd stir it right in. A teaspoon or two. Maybe more. Arsenic doesn't change the smell. Doesn't change the taste. Most folks wouldn't suspect a thing."

Nannie herself had put it even more plainly during questioning:

"It was easy."

Investigators say she grinned when she said it.

From the victims' perspective, the process was terrible.

Arsenic poisoning didn't kill instantly. Symptoms resembled food poisoning or stomach flu—vomiting, diarrhea, cramps, weakness. In remote areas where many families lacked access to proper medical care, unexpected illness was widespread. People blamed dirty water, ruined food, and seasonal diseases.

Nannie blamed "God's will."

In Samuel's instance, his first fall sparked medical scrutiny only because he recovered. His doctor noted the violent gastrointestinal symptoms, the quick dehydration, the precipitous drop in blood pressure. The disease didn't behave like a regular infection.

"That man looked poisoned," the doctor later told investigators. "I told him plainly: something ain't right."

But after his hospital stay, Samuel went home.

And that evening, Nannie prepared him another meal.

Investigators, using autopsy reports, ultimately discovered that the dose he received next was significantly stronger—fatal within hours.

When neighbors questioned what happened, Nannie clasped her hands and whispered gently, "My poor Sammy... he just wasn't strong enough."

She giggled quietly after speaking.

No one questioned it at the time.

What investigators would subsequently learn is that this method—meals laced with arsenic—was constant across Nannie's past. In multiple states. Across several marriages. And even inside her own family.

In Alabama, her second husband, Frank Harrelson, died under circumstances so identical that the sheriff who investigated the case subsequently shook his head and said, "We should've seen it. But back then? Lots of men drank nasty moonshine, ate poor meat. Folks died young."

In North Carolina, evidence of poisoning was suspected in the untimely death of her mother, Louisa. Neighbors remembered that Nannie had been the one caring for her in her dying days, cooking all her meals and bringing warm cider in the evenings.

A relative, interviewed decades later, recalls the moment she watched Nannie bring her mother a steaming cup.

"She said, 'Here, Mama, this'll help.' Then she laughed a little. I didn't think anything of it. But now? Now I hear that chuckle differently."

In Kansas, the death of her husband Arlie Lanning raised few concerns at the time. The local narrative had been simple: Arlie drank too much. His health was worsening. His death made sense.

But when investigators reexamined the pattern, the similarities were startling. Sudden sickness. Gastrointestinal discomfort. Rapid decrease. Nannie as the caregiver.

It was a recipe repeated too many times to be a coincidence.

The forensic details became the tipping point.

When Oklahoma state pathologist Dr. A. J. McElroy conducted Samuel Doss's autopsy, he reported detecting "a large amount of arsenic" in Samuel's organs. Enough to kill a man rapidly. Enough to leave no question.

In the official report, McElroy wrote:

"This was no accidental ingestion."

For the first time, the evidence wasn't circumstantial. It was scientific. Clear. Unmistakable.

When detectives faced Nannie with the toxicological findings, she didn't cry. She didn't refute anything.

She giggled.

And then she talked.

Detectives would subsequently remember how unnerving that moment was.

"She told us which husbands she poisoned like she was reading off a grocery list," one officer claimed. "No remorse. Just… amusement."

In transcripts, investigators noted how she referred to arsenic as "my little helper." How she indicated that adding poison into coffee or stews was straightforward. How she stated that some husbands "deserved it" for drinking or infidelity. Others, she continued, were just "no fun."

The more the cops pressed, the more details revealed.

And the clearer the pattern became:

Different states. Different husbands. Sometimes her own children or grandkids. Sometimes her mother.

But always in the same manner.

Always the same smile.

Always the giggle.

As investigators looked over the gathered deaths spanning Alabama, North Carolina, Kansas, and Oklahoma, the enormity of her crimes became inescapably evident. For years she had gone across state borders, beginning fresh after each death, leaving behind families who felt they had suffered natural catastrophes.

No one had connected the dots.

But now, every piece—every mysterious death—was coming into place.

Nannie's "kitchen kindness."
Her persistent attendance at the bedside.
Her desire to serve meals and drinks.
Her deceptively soft laugh.

It wasn't kindness.

It was a ritual.

A process perfected over decades.

And now, with her confession on record and forensic proof in hand, investigators were set to unravel the full extent of her poisoning binge.

The next chapter would describe how the truth eventually broke through the illusion—and how the police caught up to the woman who masked murder behind a smile.

Chapter 5

Victims Close to Home

The tragedy of Nannie Doss's story was not simply the scale of her crimes—but the proximity of them. Most serial killers avoid harming the people closest to them.

Nannie did not.

The people who trusted her most—the ones who shared her kitchen, her table, her bed—were generally the first to fall victim. Each death appeared solitary, terrible, believable. But collectively, they formed a chain of wordless screams that no one heard until it was too late.

The earliest remembered casualty was her own young granddaughter.

In 1945, Nannie's daughter, Florine, had recently given birth. Family relatives recalled Nannie being especially involved—hovering, fussing, insisting on assisting with the infant even when Florine maintained she was fine.

One evening, Florine would later recount to investigators:

"Mama said she'd rock the baby to sleep. I didn't think twice. She seemed so cheerful, singing and grinning like she often did."

Hours later, the infant died abruptly.

Doctors labeled it asphyxiation... or potentially an unknown sickness. Infant deaths were heartbreakingly common at the time.

No one blamed Nannie.

But years later, as police lined up the timeline, this death—quiet, unnoticed—became one of the first red lights in a long trail.

Her spouses followed a very similar pattern.

Charlie Braggs, her first husband, survived her—but very barely. After years of marital instability, he abandoned the house, taking their oldest daughter with him. As police tracked him down decades later, his voice still conveyed vibrations as he spoke of those years.

"I knew something wasn't right," he claimed. "Her moods... they changed like the weather. And stuff kept happenin'. Folks became sick. Her family... my mama..." His voice cracked. "I had to get out."

Charlie didn't have evidence. Only fear. But terror kept him alive.

Others were not as fortunate.

Robert Harrelson, spouse number two, was the kind of man who worked hard and drank harder. His constant drinking made him susceptible, and Nannie utilized that to disguise what she eventually admitted doing.

In a reconstruction based on family interviews, the last evening of his life occurred in a darkly lighted living room, radio crackling gently.

"Nannie," he whispered, collapsed in a chair, "you're too good to me."

She giggled in response, placing a warm drink in his hands.

He never knew what was in it.

When neighbors learned he died suddenly, they shrugged. "Frank drank himself to death," they added. "It was bound to happen."

Except it wasn't drinking that killed him.

It was arsenic.

Arlie Lanning, husband number three, died in North Carolina. His death certificate indicated heart failure—understandable for a man who smoked regularly and lived a rough life. The community united behind Nannie. She cried convincingly. She made casseroles for the funeral personnel. She accepted condolences gracefully.

But Arlie's sister always had reservations.

In an interview, she recalled:

"There was something off. Arlie had his difficulties, certainly, but he wasn't that sick. And Nannie... she didn't appear surprised. Just acted like she'd expected it."

Investigators later found arsenic in his system—but only after tying him to the bigger pattern.

The killings began to hit even closer when Nannie went inward—toward her own blood.

Her mother, Louisa Hazel, died after only a few days of Nannie caring for her. The way doctors saw it, elderly individuals usually died of acute illness.

But Florine—Nannie's daughter—would later disclose a recollection that troubled her.

"Mama brought Grandma a bowl of warm oatmeal," she remarked. "She was smiling, saying, 'Eat up, Mama, you need strength.' Grandma ate it, and Mama just watched… quiet. Then she giggled a little. I inquired what was funny, and she answered, 'Oh, nothing honey.'"

Hours later, Louisa was dead.

Florine didn't question it at the moment.

"Now I wish I had," she muttered in the interview.

The web widened.

Her sister died under similar circumstances.

A nephew experienced a sudden, unexplained illness immediately after eating one of Nannie's dishes but survived by sheer luck.

And then there was the case that truly shattered the chain: Samuel Doss, the man who trusted her most, the polite churchgoing spouse who read self-help books and believed in doing everything the appropriate way.

His suspicious illness—and recovery—alerted his doctor.

His untimely second death caused the autopsy.

And his autopsy exposed the truth.

Detectives working the Samuel Doss investigation revealed the moment they began connecting earlier deaths.

Lieutenant Bill Bristow laid old obituaries and medical records across his desk: infants, children, husbands, a mother, a sister. All from various states. All related to the same woman.

"These can't all be coincidences," he whispered.

His partner flipped over a study listing symptoms associated with arsenic poisoning.

"Look at this," the partner said. "Every one of these victims showed the same signs—vomiting, stomach pain, sudden collapse."

Bristow leaned back, inhaling slowly.

"My God... how long has she been doing this? "

They didn't have enough evidence to exhume every former victim. Some graves were too old, some families rejected, and some states lacked jurisdiction.

But the pattern—once invisible—now flashed like a warning sign.

As detectives pulled together data, a disturbing conclusion emerged: nearly every fatality occurred when Nannie was in the home, caring for the sufferer, making meals, pouring drinks, or offering warm "comforting" tonic.

The timeline was undeniable.
The procedure was consistent.
The access was always there.

And the deaths always ceased when Nannie went.

It was a wonderful pattern—hidden in plain sight.

The story of victim after victim—all related by family, marriage, or trust—formed the emotional center of the investigation.

They were not strangers. They were not random targets.

They were her family.
Her lovers.
Her children and grandchildren.

Victims so close that questioning her motivations felt like betrayal to those who survived.

But betrayal was etched into every motion she made. Every meal she served. Every sweet laugh.

And now, detectives had unearthed the truth: the common thread wasn't coincidence.

It was Nannie.

And the next phase would show the motive—or absence of one—that made her crimes even more troubling. A reason no one predicted, and many still struggle to grasp.

Chapter 6

Investigation Begins

The case truly began—not in a police station, not in a lab, not in a courtroom—but in a quiet hospital room in Tulsa, Oklahoma.

Samuel Doss lay on a narrow white bed, his face pale, his respiration shallow. His doctor, Dr. A. J. McKelroy stood over him, flipping through his chart, frowning in silence. Something about Samuel's symptoms didn't make sense. Violent vomiting. Sudden collapse. Severe gastric distress. A near-death episode… followed by fast improvement.

Then he went home.

And within days, he was dead.

Dr. McKelroy knew sicknesses did not act like that.

He snapped the chart shut.

"This is not a stomach virus," he murmured.

Those six words launched the entire investigation.

Detective Earl Weaver was the first officer dispatched to Samuel's residence. He strolled into the living room where Nannie sat on the couch, clothed elegantly, hands folded in her lap. She had her normal lovely smile. A Bible sat near her.

"Mrs. Doss, I'm sorry for your loss," Weaver replied, softly easing into the interview.

"Oh, thank you, officer," she said sweetly, tucking a curl behind her ear. "Samuel was a good man. The Lord just decided it was time."

Weaver observed her intently. Most widows trembled. Most cried. Many couldn't speak at all.
But Nannie smiled.
She giggled beneath her breath.

Weaver made a note of it.

"Mind telling me about his final hours?" he said.

"Oh, well…" she began, and her tone got lighter, almost happy. "He just wasn't feeling himself. I made him some coffee. He enjoyed my coffee."

Coffee.
The same drink Samuel's doctor cautioned him to avoid after his first odd illness.

Weaver's eyebrows lifted.

"And after he drank the coffee?" he pressed.

"He went to lie down. And… well… the Good Lord took him in his sleep."
Another giggle.

Weaver's instincts sharpened. Something was wrong. He left the house uncomfortable, whispering to his partner:

"She's hiding something. And that ain't grief."

The turning point came at the Oklahoma State Laboratory.

The autopsy on Samuel Doss was normal at first—until the toxicologist, Dr. A. J. McElroy analyzed the stomach contents and tissue samples. His aide observed as he adjusted the chemical reagent.

Within seconds, a visible discoloration appeared.

McElroy stiffened.

"Run that again," he urged.

They repeated the test.
Same result.
Clear. Consistent.

"Arsenic," McElroy muttered. "And a lot of it."

He removed his spectacles, massaged his eyes, and peered at the report forming in front of him.

"This wasn't accidental ingestion," he wrote.
"This was deliberate poisoning."

He immediately contacted the police.

Detective Weaver and Sheriff Bill Bristow were at the lab within hours.

McElroy slid the paper across the table.

"That man was poisoned with arsenic," he continued.

Weaver scanned down the list of toxicological findings.

"Enough to kill him twice," McElroy added.

Weaver breathed slowly.
"Then we're not looking at a natural death," he stated.
He turned to Bristow. "We need to bring her in."

The first formal interview was done inside a tiny room at the Tulsa police station. Nannie strolled in wearing a floral dress and a soft pink cardigan. She smiled cheerfully at the cops.

"You boys need me for something?" she inquired.

Bristow motioned for her to sit.

"Mrs. Doss, we received the toxicology results."

"Oh?" Her eyebrows raised playfully.

"We found arsenic in Samuel's system."

There was a long delay.

Then she giggled—lightly, almost childlike.

"Oh my," she responded, "is that so?"

Weaver leaned forward.

"Nannie… did you put anything in his food? In his drink?"

"Oh no, honey," she said sweetly. "I only ever tried to make him comfortable. I loved him—everyone knows that."

Weaver shared a gaze with Bristow.
Her charisma was almost choreographed.
Her calm is disconcerting.

Bristow tried a new angle.

"Mind if we talk to your family, Mrs. Doss? Just to realize what kind of man Samuel was."

"Well, sure," she answered with a pleasant shrug. "Talk to whoever you like."

She had no fear.
Not yet.

Detectives next visited Nannie's relatives. One by one, cracks in the story began to surface.

Nannie's daughter Florine shuffled uncomfortably in her seat when quizzed.

"I don't wanna believe anything bad about Mama," she muttered. "But… well… people have died around her. A lot of people."

"What do you mean?" Weaver asked kindly.

Florine hesitated.

"My baby girl… died suddenly after Mama fed her." Her voice broke. "I didn't think anything of it. Now I don't know."

Other families echoed similar stories: abrupt illnesses, inexplicable deaths, and Nannie constantly nearby… cooking, caring, offering drinks and warm meals.

A neighbor from North Carolina recalled:

"Arlie dropped dead out of nowhere, and Nannie acted… relieved. Not sad. Relieved."

A granddaughter spoke in a weak voice:

"Mama said Grandma's food always tasted funny. Bitter. Weird."

The detectives carefully logged every statement.

Piece by piece, a terrifying pattern was developing.

The second breakthrough occurred when Weaver obtained death information from other places where Nannie had lived.

Alabama.
North Carolina.
Kansas.

The records came in large envelopes, heaped on Bristow's desk like a gloomy repository.

Every death certificate told a same story:

Sudden sickness.
Gastrointestinal failure.
Cardiac arrest.
No suspicion of foul play.

Bristow frowned at the list of causes.

"These look like arsenic symptoms," he mumbled.

Weaver nodded slowly.

"And every one of those people died while she was in the home."

They labored late into the night, connecting dots across decades and geographies.

"Six husbands," Weaver answered gently.

"And nearly every one died," Bristow finished.

"But not just husbands," Weaver emphasized. "Family. Children. Grandchildren. Her mother."

Silence engulfed the room.

Bristow murmured, "This is bigger than we thought."

The investigators returned to Nannie with what they had. She sat in the interview room, hands folded nicely.

Weaver placed a file in front of her.

"These are death records from Alabama, Tennessee, North Carolina, and Kansas. People close to you."

Nannie inclined her head, smiling.

"Oh my… that's quite a stack."

"We know about the arsenic," he replied quietly.

Another giggle.

"And we believe Samuel wasn't your only victim."

This time, Nannie's smile faltered—just slightly.

Weaver leaned closer, voice low, steady:

"How many people have died... because of you?"

There was a long stillness.
So long that the investigators worried if she would ever answer.

Then she moaned quietly.

"Well," she began, almost sweetly, "it all started... a long time ago."

Weaver froze.

Bristow stared at her.

She wasn't denying it.
She was reminiscing.

And that told them everything.

They weren't dealing with a heartbroken widow.

They were dealing with a serial poisoner.

Possibly one of the deadliest ladies in American history.

And the next chapter would reveal her whole confession—and the terrifying motivations behind her lethal laughter.

Chapter 7

Confessions and Revelations

The questioning room at the Tulsa courthouse was colder than normal that October morning in 1954. Fluorescent lights hummed overhead. A metal chair scraped the floor as Detective Ray Porter sat down opposite Nannie Doss—a little woman draped in a floral print dress, hands folded neatly, smiling like she'd just strolled in for a church interview rather than a homicide interrogation.

The press would subsequently call her smile "ghoulish" and "unnerving."
But at that moment, it was simply… continuous.

The detective opened with facts—dates, death certificates, strange patterns. He expected opposition. He expected tears. He expected denial.

He got a giggle.

A quiet, almost happy giggle that resonated through the walls.

The same laugh had captivated neighbors, diverted nurses, and won over bereaved relatives for decades. And here, in a space created for truth, it twisted into something terrible.

"Mrs. Doss," Porter continued slowly, "we're asking about the death of your husband, Samuel Doss."

Nannie tilted her head. "Poor Sam," she whispered. "He was a good man. Too tight, yet good."

"You remarried him after he fell ill the first time," Porter added. "Doctors said it was unusual—violent stomach pains, vomiting, nervous system collapse. Then he dies right after you bring him something to eat."

Another giggle.

"People die," Nannie said carelessly. "That's life."

But Porter had the advantage no small-town coroner ever did: a laboratory test confirming high arsenic concentration in Sam's organs. The toxicology report rested on the table between them, ink still fresh.

He slid it toward her.

Nannie leaned in, eyes narrowing briefly, as if scrutinizing embroidery on a quilt. Then she shrugged.

"I didn't mean for Sam to suffer," she claimed.

The detective's pen froze mid-air.

The room shifted.

Nannie Doss had just stepped over the line between suspicion and admission.

Porter swallowed. "Are you saying you poisoned your husband?"

Nannie lifted her hands slowly, the giggle bubbling up again. "Well," she said, "I reckon sometimes a woman has to do things. A girl gets tired, you know."

Her voice was almost playful—an aunt whispering a family secret at Thanksgiving, not a woman confessing to murder.

"Tell us everything," Porter said quietly.

What followed stunned even the seasoned investigators.

She didn't just talk about Sam.
She went back years.

She talked about Frank, who drank too much.
She talked about Arlie, who cheated.
She talked about her mother.
Her sister.
Her grandchildren.

Each confession dropped like a stone in water—ripples of disbelief filling the room.

"I fixed Frank's whiskey," she said matter-of-factly. "He was mean when he drank. I didn't like that."

Detective Sanders, who had been observing from the corner, shifted uncomfortably. "Fix it how?"

"With that powder," she replied. "The rat poison."

"You kept arsenic in the house?"

"Land sakes, every woman did. For bugs. For pests."

"For husbands?" Porter asked.

She laughed harder this time—high-pitched, breathless, a sound investigators would later describe as "the most disturbing thing in the entire case."

When they asked about Arlie, she gave a little sigh. "Arlie was a bad man. Ran around too much. I put bug poison in his coffee. He loved his coffee."

"And your mother?" Sanders whispered.

Nannie paused. For the first time, the smile faltered.

"She was sick," she said. "I just helped her rest."

The detectives exchanged glances. She'd admitted to multiple husbands, but this—her own blood—cut deeper.

"How many people, Nannie?" Porter asked quietly.

She tapped her fingers on the table. "Hmm. I don't know. Quite a few, I suppose."

Her tone was chillingly casual.

The confession lasted hours. Investigators flipped through pages of notes, each line more surreal than the last. What struck them wasn't just the quantity of prospective victims—but her apparent lack of guilt.

At one point, a stenographer entered the room. She froze as she heard Nannie cheerfully discussing her ways.

"I'd slip a bit in their food," Nannie said, miming the sprinkling motion. "Or in their drinks. Or prune cake—prune cake works real good."

The stenographer's hands shook so badly she nearly dropped her notepad.

Outside the interrogation room, reporters crowded hallways, scribbling headlines the moment whispers leaked out:

THE GIGGLING GRANNY CONFESSES SMILING SERIAL KILLER ADMITS MULTIPLE MURDERS BLACK WIDOW FROM OKLAHOMA LAUGHS THROUGH INTERROGATION

Editorials questioned how a woman—an elderly, soft-spoken, cookie-baking grandmother—could be responsible for such evil. Historians later noted that mid-century America struggled to comprehend the idea of a female serial killer, especially one who looked like she belonged in a church choir.

But Nannie didn't care about public astonishment.

During one break, as detectives stepped out, she leaned back in her chair, humming softly, almost content. When Sanders re-entered, she smiled at him, as if he were an old friend bringing her pie.

"You know," she continued sweetly, "I never hurt anyone who didn't make me unhappy."

He stared at her. "You killed them, Nannie."

She shrugged. "Well, unhappiness is murder too."

When the confession videos rolled, she talked freely—almost eagerly—about her techniques, her motives, her frustrations with men who failed her romantic fantasies. She quoted love magazine columns. She speculated about marriage being "disappointing" and "a burden." She spoke about "cleaning up messes."

Every giggle was captured on tape.

By the end of the confession, detectives were left drained, horrified, and overwhelmed with a dreadful realization:

Nannie Doss hadn't merely committed murder.
She had relished the strength of it.
She had relished the show of admitting.

And she had relished witnessing the fear emerge on the faces of men who thought they understood evil.

When the tapes clicked off, Porter sat back, fatigued.

"Nannie," he replied, scratching his temples, "do you understand the seriousness of what you've told us?"

She grinned brightly.

"Oh, don't fuss," she chirped. "I'm ready to go wherever you need me."

Outside, the media frenzy grew as news surfaced that the laughing grandma from Oklahoma wasn't simply a heartbroken widow—she was one of America's most prolific female serial killers.

And yet… This was merely the beginning.
Her trial, her infamy, the country's collective shock—none of it could properly contain the horrific reality she had so nonchalantly disclosed in that frigid interrogation room.

Nannie Doss had giggled her way through life.
Now, she was chuckling her way through confession.

And the world was finally listening.

Chapter 8

Psychological Profile

When the confessions ended and the legal machinery took over, another team stepped in—quiet, clinical, curious. Criminologists, psychologists, and behavioral analysts wanted something the detectives couldn't give them:

An understanding of the woman behind the giggle.

In a small consultation room inside the Oklahoma State Hospital, Dr. Margaret Holbrook reviewed the growing file on Nannie Doss. It was thick—confessions, marriage records, coroner reports, letters she'd written to lonely-hearts columns, and transcripts from her interrogation.

Holbrook adjusted her glasses, whispering to herself, "How does a grandmother poison half her family and still get described as 'sweet'?"

She turned the page. A quote from a neighbor caught her eye:

"Nannie was a joy. Always smiling. Always laughing."

Holbrook circled that sentence.

Charm.
A weapon as powerful as arsenic.

A flashback flickered across Holbrook's mind—constructed from witness statements and Nannie's own admissions:

Nannie in her kitchen, humming as she stirred a pot. Her face is calm. Focused.
A teaspoon of something white gliding through the air.
A soft whisper to herself: "Just enough, not too much."

Holbrook scribbled on her notepad.

Predatory calm. No emotional arousal during the act.

Most female murderers are killed in moments of panic, desperation, or prolonged abuse. But Nannie was poisoned with patience. With calculation. With a smile.

A rare type.

A chilling one.

In another office across the building, forensic psychiatrist Dr. Alan Wexler listened to the taped confession again—the one where she giggled through describing how she sprinkled arsenic into her husband's coffee.

"She enjoys the memory," he muttered. "Not just the control. The retelling."

He paused the tape.

This wasn't typical psychopathy.
This wasn't typical sociopathy.

This was something… fused.

A lifetime of romantic fantasy—cheap love-story magazines, dreams of perfect men, escapism born from childhood trauma—colliding with a violent internal logic:

If a man disappoints me, he doesn't deserve to live.

A therapist might have called it cognitive distortion.

A prosecutor would call it motive.
A criminologist saw it as a pattern.

Wexler pressed play again.

Nannie's voice filled the room, light and airy:
"Well, he made me really unhappy. And when I get unhappy, I just fix the problem."

Wexler shivered.

Holbrook later interviewed surviving friends and acquaintances. Every story repeated the same adjectives: polite, cheerful, affectionate, funny.

The giggle—always the giggle.

A church lady recalled, "She'd bring pies to potlucks. She'd laugh and joke. Who'd suspect her of anything?"

Holbrook underlined the note:

High social masking ability.

Serial killers often showed coldness, irritability, and emotional flatness. Nannie? She was warm. Engaging. Endearing.

Holbrook explained later in a lecture:

> "She disarmed suspicion through maternal stereotypes. She weaponized femininity. Her charm created a psychological blind spot in those around her—making her one of the most dangerous types of offenders."

Interviewer: "So the charm wasn't accidental?"

Holbrook: "No. It was cultivated."

As analysts continued their work, they created a psychological reconstruction of her internal world—pieced together from interviews, confession tapes, letters, and the chilling consistency of her behavior.

At night, Nannie would sit alone at her kitchen table.
Her thoughts were an echo chamber of grievances and fantasies:

He doesn't appreciate me.

He promised he'd stop drinking.

He should be better.

I could make things better.

Punchy internal monologue. Short, sharp, morally warped.

In several documented cases, relatives recalled her speaking softly to herself after an argument, as if rehearsing a justification:

"He brought this on himself."

"They all disappoint me sooner or later."

"A good man shouldn't cause a woman such trouble."

These weren't momentary frustrations—they were rehearsed rationalizations.
Rehearsals for murder.

When Dr. Holbrook analyzed these patterns, she wrote in her report:

> "Her worldview is anchored in entitlement and emotional self-preservation. If someone disturbs her psychological comfort, she eliminates the source. Her giggling is not joy—it is deflection, disassociation, and at times, pleasure."

The criminologists also compared Nannie to other known female serial killers of the era.

Belle Gunness, the "Black Widow of La Porte," killed for financial gain.
Juana Barraza, decades later in Mexico, killed elderly women with brute force—rage-driven, not methodical.
Jane Toppan, the nurse who confessed to killing dozens with morphine, had a sadistic streak tied to medical access.

Nannie fit her own category.

A cocktail of motives:
Romantic disappointment. Financial convenience. Revenge. Control. Fantasy.

But three things made her unique:

1. She killed across multiple states—leaving behind a trail rarely connected until toxicology exposed the pattern.

2. She used poison almost exclusively, maintaining a feminine, nonviolent method that shielded her from suspicion.

3. She smiled through everything—even during confession.

Holbrook summarized it best:

> "She hid in plain sight by becoming exactly what society expected a grandmother to be. No one looked behind the laugh."

During a joint review session, Wexler played a short clip from the confession tapes for a group of assembled criminologists. The room was silent as Nannie's high-pitched giggle filled the speaker system.

Then her voice—soft, sweet, horrifying:

"I guess I just liked the quiet after they were gone."

A few of the experts flinched.

Holbrook turned off the recorder.

"She's not describing relief," she said. "She's describing satisfaction."

Wexler nodded. "And she wants us to know."

That was the part that unsettled them most.

Nannie didn't brag, but she didn't hide.
She didn't gloat, but she didn't regret.
She simply recounted the murders as if they were chores, done with practiced domestic efficiency.

She wanted the world to hear her giggle—and wonder what it meant.

In the final section of the psychological report, Holbrook wrote a line that would later be quoted in documentaries and textbooks:

> "Understanding Nannie Doss requires understanding the duality of her existence—half romance, half ruin. The grandmother and the predator. The laughter and the poison."

And yet, even with the analysis, even with the confessions, even with her unsettling calm, one question lingered among the experts:

How many victims were there really?

She confessed to some.
Investigators suspected many more.
Coroners could confirm only a few.

The rest were lost to time, to incomplete records, to untested remains.

A mystery wrapped in a smile.

A darkness hidden behind a giggle.

And in that uncertainty—in that space where facts end and fear begins—the fascination with Nannie Doss continues to grow, decade after decade.

Because she wasn't just a killer.

She was a reminder that evil doesn't always snarl.

Sometimes… it laughs.

Chapter 9

Media and Myth

The morning after Nannie Doss's confession became public, the country woke to bold, black headlines splashed across front pages from Oklahoma to New York.

"THE GIGGLING GRANNY ADMITS TO MULTIPLE POISONINGS."
"SMILING SERIAL KILLER: GRANDMOTHER TELLS ALL."
"BLACK WIDOW LAUGHS THROUGH CONFESSION."

In crowded newsrooms across America, typewriters clattered like machine-gun fire. Cigarette smoke swirled heavily over reporters as they shouted across desks cluttered with coffee cups, police blotters, and telegram wires.

"Get me a quote from the sheriff!"
"Double-check the number—was it nine victims or eleven?"
"Find a neighbor willing to talk!"

The case wasn't just news.
It was a spectacle.

A grandmother—round-faced, soft-voiced, laughing as she admitted to poisoning her husbands?
It was the kind of story editors knew would fly off newsstands.

In one newsroom, a young reporter named Clarence James slapped the morning edition onto his desk and stared at her picture. She looked so harmless, so ordinary.

He muttered to his colleague, "She looks like someone who'd bake you a pie."

His colleague said, "Yeah. Then she'd poison it."

They both chuckled uneasily, but neither noticed the chill that followed.

Press conferences became chaotic. Cameramen pushed forward. Journalists jostled elbows. Microphones captured every word the investigators said—even when those words didn't reveal much.

"Is it true she confessed to killing all four husbands?"
"Why was no one suspicious before?"
"Did she giggle during the confession?"
"Is she insane?"

Reporters wanted color, drama, emotion.
And Nannie delivered.

At one point, when brought into the courthouse, she turned to a camera and remarked, "Smile now—don't make me look bad."

The giggle followed.
Light. Carefree.
Terrifying.

Photographers later admitted that hearing it in person unsettled them more than reading about her crimes.

One journalist wrote, "Her eyes smiled before her mouth did. That was the strange part."

As the coverage intensified, the nation started building a myth around her.

People traded stories at barbershops, beauty salons, and church gatherings.

"I heard she poisoned her babies."
"I heard she used rat poison in the biscuits."
"I heard she'd been killing since she was a teenager."
"I heard she danced after each murder."

Most of it wasn't true.
Some of it was… uncomfortably close.

But truth rarely survives public curiosity.

Nannie had become a character—a legend—long before the courts concluded anything.

Radio broadcasters dramatized her life:

"…and in the quiet kitchen, the widow slipped arsenic into the coffee cup…"

Some stations produced reenactments with actresses giggling on cue, their voices pitched high to mimic her eerie lightness.

Listeners sat in their living rooms, leaning closer to their radios as if hearing the giggle directly through the speakers.

Newspapers published sketches of her as the ultimate black widow, draped in dark clothing with sinister smiles. The real Nannie wore floral dresses and bobby pins, but accuracy mattered far less than entertainment.

Detectives hated this.

One investigator told a reporter, "This isn't a movie. We're dealing with genuine deaths, real victims."

The reporter nodded, then went back to creating his next headline.

Years later, when true crime blossomed into a cultural fascination, Nannie Doss re-emerged again and again.
Documentaries dissected her methods.
Books retold her marriages and murders.
Television adaptations cast actresses with sweet smiles and soft voices.

The contrast was compelling.
A grandmother who killed with a laugh.

Shows called her:
The Jolly Poisoner.
The Merry Widow.
The Giggling Granny.

Producers leaned toward the irony—playing up her giggle, highlighting her floral outfits, juxtaposing innocence with terror.

But the dramatizations blurred lines.
Scenes imagined talks she never had.
Episodes exaggerated motivations.
Some productions stated she relished watching her victims suffer.
Others stated she chatted to herself in the mirror.
One even pictured her dancing through a kitchen loaded with poison bottles placed like trophies.

None of that was documented.

But they believed it.

Holbrook, the criminologist from the previous chapter, once stated in a lecture that the media had essentially transformed Nannie into a symbol—a parody of the "female serial killer" paradigm.

"She became the perfect storm of what the public fears," Holbrook added. "A trusted figure. A caretaker. A woman who used domesticity as a mask."

In trying to understand her, the media mythologized her.

Meanwhile, the real Nannie languished in prison, reading newspaper cuttings brought to her by guards. According to sources, she found some of the coverage humorous.

"She laughed at the cartoons of herself," one guard recounted. "Said they made her look too skinny."

Another guard recalls her reaction to a radio dramatization: "She said the actress didn't laugh right."

She wasn't angry.
She wasn't defensive.
She found the spectacle entertaining.

To her, it was all a performance she no longer needed to hide behind.

But as rumors circulated, investigators were concerned that the myth was overshadowing the reality. Families of victims felt erased, their tragedies reduced to headlines.

One relative spoke to a reporter: "They talk about her like she's a character. But she killed real people. My people."

The reporter included the quote—but hid it beneath a more spectacular subheading.

By the 1960s, Nannie's narrative had entered American legend.

By the 1980s, true-crime novelists carried it further.

By the 2000s, internet forums analyzed her like a puzzle.

By the 2010s, documentary filmmakers reframed her as one of the earliest proto-female serial killers in U.S. history.

Truth and myth twisted together until they became virtually indistinguishable.

And still, one question refused to fade:

How many victims were never identified?

Investigators had their suspicions.

Historians have their theories.

Her confession revealed glimpses but not totals.

One investigator who worked the case once remarked quietly, "We'll never know the real number."

And he wasn't the only one who thought so.

Because beneath the press frenzy, beyond the fantastic re-tellings, behind the headlines and documentary voiceovers, there remained a final, terrifying possibility—

The full narrative of Nannie Doss might yet be incomplete.

A cliff just barely visible.

A shadow hiding something deeper.

And the next chapter—the next revelation—was waiting on the brink of that darkness.

Ready to expose exactly how much the world still didn't know.

Chapter 10

Societal Reflections

The story of Nannie Doss didn't end with her confession, nor with the headlines that labeled her the Giggling Granny.
In many ways, it began there.

Because once the laughing faded and the facts settled, society had to face an uncomfortable truth:

She wasn't just a killer.
She was a reflection—distorted, unsettling—of the blind spots America carried for decades.

The documentary crew interviewing criminologist Dr. Lena Gray set up the lights, capturing her silhouette against a stark white backdrop. When the cameras rolled, Gray leaned forward, hands folded, voice quiet.

"People didn't see her coming," she claimed. "And that wasn't an accident. It was cultural."

She tapped the table with her pen.

"Women weren't supposed to kill. Grandmothers least of all."

A pause.

"That stereotype helped her."

Flashback—reconstructed from interviews and testimony:

Nannie donned an apron, hummed sweetly as she put a tablecloth across a wooden table. A pot bubbled on the burner. The kitchen sparkled in warm tones. A spouse sat nearby, coughing lightly, ignorant of what swirled in his coffee cup.

This scene—so commonplace, so domestic—was exactly why investigators of the 1940s and 1950s failed to view her as a threat.

Dr. Gray's voice superimposed over the scene:

"In that era, domesticity was the safest space. A woman's place. If someone died at home, people assumed disease, not murder. Especially not murder by a pleasant, friendly wife."

When the memory ended, the camera moved to commentator Michael Reeves, a historian specialized in American culture.

"She weaponized the role," Reeves said. "She used the home—the very symbol of comfort—as her stage."

He shook his head, almost in amazement.

"And society applauded her performance until it was far too late."

Court transcripts suggest investigators first rejected concerns voiced by a relative.
The doctor overseeing one husband's death scribbled "heart failure" without suspecting a thing.
Neighbors blamed bad luck, stress, or "something going around."

The blind spot wasn't simply social—it was systemic.

Detective Harris, an aging man in the final interview he ever gave, explained it plainly:

"She was a grandmother. Sweet. Polite. We didn't consider poison at first because... well... we didn't consider her."

Domestic evil.
That's what some commentators later dubbed it.

The silent kind.
The unseen kind.

The kind that dwells behind lace curtains, floral gowns, and pleasant smiles.

The footage moves to a theatrical montage: —Nannie rocking in a chair, sewing.
— A husband complains of stomach aches.
— A child knocks on her door for cookies. — A neighbor waving as she tended her roses.

All scenes drawn from genuine accounts.

Over it, a narrator reflects:

"She killed the people closest to her. The folks who trusted her most. Not with a weapon of aggression, but with one of routine. Caregiving evolved into control. Domesticity turned into death."

In the next interview, psychologist Dr. Yvonne Fletcher explains:

"Her murders happened in the spaces where women were expected to be nurturing. That paradox is part of what makes her case so unsettling. She converted the safest space into the most dangerous."

She paused.

"And she smiled while doing it."

But the case didn't only affect the way society regarded household roles—it exposed vulnerabilities in law enforcement systems.

Toxicology testing in rural hospitals during the 1940s and early 1950s was uneven.
Coroners typically didn't test for arsenic.
Serial poisoning was rarely suspected unless victims had enemies or financial disputes—and even then, suspicion fell on men.

The documentary switches to an archival interview with forensic analyst Dr. Leonard Keane:

"It was her last husband's sudden death that finally raised suspicion. But when we analyzed the tissue samples—so much arsenic… it was undeniable."

He gazed down, still disturbed decades later.

"Looking back, the signs were there earlier. We just didn't link them."

Modern detectives routinely use the Nannie Doss case when training new police and forensic techs.
Her crimes underscored the necessity for pattern recognition across jurisdictions.
She was killed in numerous states—Alabama, North Carolina, Oklahoma, possibly more.

"No one compared notes," a veteran FBI analyst explained in a recent interview.
"Back then, information didn't move the way it does now. If it had? She wouldn't have progressed as far as she did."

The documentary flashes a timeline graphic on screen—deaths mapped across years and state lines—each one initially considered to be natural.

A disturbing reminder of how readily patterns can lie in plain sight.

But the societal reflections didn't end with institutional failings.

Commentators highlighted another reality: Nannie's cheery manner disarmed practically everyone.

Photos show her smiling—wide, comfortable, almost radiant—during press briefings.

A reporter at the time wrote, "Her giggle was disarming. It made you forget what she did."

The documentary investigates this duality: How appeal covers danger.
How look influences suspicion.
How stereotypes shape justice.

One scene shows criminologist Dr. Gray pointing to a photograph of Nannie.

"A killer doesn't always look like a killer. And a granny isn't always harmless."

As the chapter nears its end, the narrative switches back to a final dramatized domestic scene—one taken straight from statements made by a surviving relative.

Nannie looks at a window, watching neighborhood children play in the yard next door.
She holds a cup of coffee, her reflection slightly visible in the glass.
The corners of her mouth twist upward—an expression impossible to read.
Fondness?
Fatigue?
Something darker?

A neighbor, heard in voiceover from an interview decades later, says:

"She seemed sweet. Just sweet. Until she wasn't."

The camera cuts to black.

And in the silence that follows, a narrator delivers the haunting truth:

"When society looked at Nannie Doss, it saw a grandmother. It didn't see a killer. Her story requires us to confront not just what she did—but what we failed to see. And how easy it could happen again."

The screen disappears, leaving the reader with a faint, crawling tension.

Because some reflections don't disclose the monster.

Some reflections reveal us instead.

Chapter 11

Trial and Conviction

The courthouse in Oklahoma felt colder than January winter, though the radiators hissed and the sun pressed against the windows. Reporters crowded the hallway, typewriters ready, pencils sharpened, notebooks pulled open like hungry mouths waiting to eat whatever statement the prosecution delivered. Everyone had come to see her.

Nannie Doss walked in smiling.

The same soft, grandmotherly smile that had fooled neighbors across four states. The same smile she wore when police arrested her, when the cameras flashed, when she admitted without trembling that she had poisoned her fifth husband, Samuel Doss. She wore it even now as she brushed a gloved hand over her coat and nodded politely to the bailiff. If not for the heavy guard surrounding her, she could have passed for a woman attending a church luncheon.

Inside the courtroom, the tension tightened like a pulled wire.

The prosecution began with a quiet confidence. They didn't need theatrics; they had facts—cold, scientific, and undeniable. Arsenic. Enough to kill a horse. Enough found in Samuel Doss's body to erase any theory of natural death. Enough to connect this gentle-looking woman to a trail of graves stretching from Alabama to Kansas to North Carolina and finally to Oklahoma.

The defense sat stiffly, eyes darting across the room as if searching for a miracle. Their only hope was her demeanor—sweet, polite, soft-spoken. But even that charm, once her most powerful weapon, now seemed sinister under the courtroom lights.

Detective Melvin Hadel was the first major witness. He stepped into the box, his jaw tight, his voice steady but edged with disbelief that still hadn't left him since the investigation began.
"She laughed," he said, eyes fixed on the jury. "When we asked her why she did it, she laughed. Said she was 'tired of his nonsense' and wanted peace."

A murmur rippled through the gallery. Pens scratched. Typewriter keys clacked. Headlines were practically writing themselves.

THE GIGGLING GRANNY TAKES THE STAND
SMILING WIDOW ADMITS TO POISONING
BLACK WIDOW LAUGHS ABOUT DEATH

On cue, the camera flashes brightened the room like lightning.

The prosecution continued: bottles, letters, love poems she clipped from magazines, insurance documents, arsenic purchases, testimonies from previous doctors who had questioned sudden deaths but never had enough evidence to act. The jury listened, stone-faced, shifting only when photographs of victims were passed around. They saw the hollow eyes of men who trusted her, children she had babysat, relatives who never suspected danger.

When Nannie chose to speak, the room almost held its breath.

She didn't cry. She didn't tremble. She didn't deny anything.
"I liked romance," she said softly, fingers intertwined, voice steady. "But men... men disappointed me."

A juror flinched.

The prosecutor stepped forward. "And your solution, Mrs. Doss?"

She lifted one shoulder—a light, effortless shrug. Something almost girlish.

"Arsenic worked."

Gasps, whispers, a journalist dropping a pen—every sound amplified beneath the vaulted ceiling.

Throughout the hearings, her calm unnerved everyone. During recess she hummed. During testimonies she smiled. When the judge sternly reminded her of the gravity of the charges, she nodded politely as though being scolded for forgetting a casserole in the oven.

Reporters leaned into their phones and whispered frantically toward their editors.
"She's smiling again—put it in the second paragraph…"
"Describe her hands—yes, tiny, delicate…"
"Get a quote from the prosecutor—this woman is chilling…"

The climax came when the forensic expert took the stand.

He described the chemical breakdown inside Samuel Doss's organs, the lethal concentration of arsenic, the unmistakable signs of deliberate poisoning. The science was irrefutable—precise, lethal, cold. The courtroom became a lab, a crime scene, a narrative that only pointed one way.

By the time closing arguments ended, the air felt thick. Even the judge seemed exhausted, worn by the weight of the crimes laid bare.

The jury took only a short time.

When they returned, every eye followed them.

Guilty.

The word landed with force. Sharp. Final.

Nannie Doss didn't blink. She simply folded her hands and nodded, the smile tugging once again at the corners of her mouth. Some swore she looked relieved. Others swore she enjoyed the attention. The prosecutor later confessed that watching her reaction unnerved him more than any confession she had given.

Sentencing followed swiftly. Life in prison.

Family members of victims cried softly in the gallery. Some prayed. Some shook their heads, caught between grief, anger, and the strange disbelief of losing loved ones to someone who looked like a grandmother handing out cookies at a church picnic.

The newspapers erupted.
"GIGGLING KILLER SENTENCED."
"SMILING SERIAL MURDERESS LOCKED AWAY FOR LIFE."
"THE BLACK WIDOW OF THE SOUTH—JUSTICE SERVED."

Inside prison walls, the myth only grew.

Guards described her as polite, cheerful, even helpful in the kitchen. She joked with inmates, told stories, wrote letters, and read romance magazines. She never expressed remorse. Not once.

Some nights she sat by her bunk and laughed softly to herself. No one ever understood why.

But the investigators who had pieced together her trail of poison knew that the smile she wore wasn't innocent. It wasn't joy. It was something darker—something that had fooled doctors, husbands, friends, neighbors, and entire communities.

As the chapter closes, we return to that smile.
The same smile she wore in court.
The same smile she carried into prison.
The same smile that left detectives wondering, even years later:

What was Nannie Doss really thinking when she killed?

And why did she always smile?

The answer, they feared, was something the world might never fully understand.

Chapter 12

Legacy and New Updates

Decades after her death in 1965, Nannie Doss continues to haunt documentaries, podcasts, and late-night true-crime discussions—her name resurfacing like a dark tide every few years when a new investigative series revisits her case. She never disappears from the cultural landscape. Instead, she lingers, smiling from grainy photographs, her eyes bright with an innocence that fooled nearly everyone she encountered.

Modern creators gravitate toward her story for one reason: she represents a contradiction wrapped in a bow. A grandmother with dimples, a soft voice, and an apron tied neatly around her waist—who murdered husbands, relatives, and children with methodical calm. That duality has become irresistible to storytellers.

In recent years, true crime podcasts have dissected her life with chilling precision. Episodes open with eerie recreations: a kettle whistling, a spoon tapping a cup, the subtle clink of arsenic crystals dissolving. Narrators whisper over soundscapes of rustling newspapers and distant sirens. Listeners, unaware of how ordinary arsenic once seemed in American homes, lean closer to their earbuds as hosts unravel the timeline—one poisoning after another, all hidden behind her warm smile.

Documentary filmmakers have also returned to her story, weaving together archival footage with modern forensic animations. Computer-rendered sequences show how arsenic ravages the body, pairing medical facts with emotional interviews from descendants of her victims. Some speak through tears; others through a generational numbness inherited from tragedy they never personally witnessed but still feel.

One recent documentary opens with a slow zoom into her most famous mugshot. As the camera approaches her eyes, the narrator murmurs, "The smile fooled a nation."

The screen cuts to a criminologist seated in a dim studio. "She was a pioneer of sorts," he says, fingers steepled. "Not because of the number of victims, but because she challenged every assumption America had about danger. We expect killers to look like monsters. She looked like your favorite aunt."

Another expert—this time a forensic psychologist—leans forward.

"Female serial killers are historically underestimated," she explains. "They often kill quietly, domestically, and strategically. Their crimes are personal, not random. Nannie Doss exemplifies this. She weaponized trust."

In panel discussions, modern academics revisit her behavioral patterns with updated terminology unavailable in the 1950s. They describe her actions as instrumental violence, narcissistic gratification, or affectless manipulation. They debate whether she sought financial gain, emotional dominance, or simply enjoyed the process of eliminating people who irritated her.

One professor summarizes:
"She found peace in death—not her own, but others'."

Across digital platforms, amateur sleuths analyze her letters, handwritings, and photographs. TikTok creators freeze-frame her smile and speculate about micro-expressions. True-crime YouTubers map her movements from state to state, overlaying timelines with eerie music. The comments sections fill with disbelief:
"How did no one suspect her?"
"She looks so sweet."
"This is terrifying."

Modern forensic experts, with tools far more advanced than anything available in the 1950s, insist she would have been caught much earlier today. Autopsy technologies, toxicology screenings, digital medical records—none of these existed during the years she quietly slipped arsenic into meals. Back then, a sudden death was often attributed to heart failure, food poisoning, or stress. Today, even subtle irregularities in bodily chemistry trigger red flags.

Yet the fascination persists not because of the science, but because of the deception.

Dramatized recreations in documentaries show her stirring a pot of stew, laughing with family, clipping magazine love stories, and waving from front porches. The scenes contrast joltingly with modern interviews from detectives who studied the case long after her death.

One retired investigator appears on screen, voice gravelly:
"She smiled too much. That's what struck me when I first read the files. Even when confessing. Even when describing how she mixed the poison. It was like she was remembering a pleasant memory."

Another modern profiler explains the deeper horror:
"She wasn't driven by rage in the traditional sense. She didn't lash out. She planned. She curated her life. If someone annoyed her or disappointed her, she quietly removed them. It's domestic homicide elevated to a pattern."

The conversation inevitably turns to gender. Society struggles to reconcile female killers with cultural ideals of motherhood, gentleness, and nurturing. When a woman commits murder—especially serial murder—it shatters the framework people rely on to understand danger.

Nannie Doss forced America to confront this uncomfortable truth:
Evil can wear a friendly face.
A killer can laugh.
A murderer can bake pies, send birthday cards, and sit knitting on a porch swing.

Her legacy lives in criminology textbooks and investigative training programs today. She is a cautionary tale used to teach officers and medical examiners never to dismiss intuition, never to accept convenient explanations, never to overlook patterns in domestic deaths—especially when one family suffers multiple tragedies.

Some modern scholars argue her story changed the way authorities approach seemingly natural deaths in homes. Others say she remains a rare anomaly, a perfect storm of opportunity, deception, and charm.

The final scenes of modern documentaries often fade out on her signature grin. Not the grin of a monster, but of someone who enjoyed the performance.

A quiet, unsettling reminder.

And that is ultimately why Nannie Doss endures. She challenges everything we believe about female violence. She blurs lines between affection and manipulation, between domestic warmth and domestic evil. Her story forces society to ask a question with no comforting answer:

If the woman next door could smile like that—and kill like that—who else might we be underestimating?

As the screen fades to black, one final line echoes—a narrator's reflective whisper meant to follow the viewer long after the credits roll:

"Her legacy isn't in the bodies she left behind, but in the fear that someone who looks harmless can hide the darkest intentions."

Latest Updates

Even decades after her death, Nannie Doss continues to captivate both investigators and audiences. In 2024–2025, a wave of new documentaries and true crime podcasts revisited her life, peeling back layers of charm and deception to examine the woman behind the infamous smile. These productions emphasized not just the murders, but the psychological games she played—how she manipulated those around her, and how communities, blinded by her grandmotherly persona, overlooked early warning signs.

Criminologists and historians highlighted the role of gendered bias in the mid-20th century. Investigators assumed women, especially grandmothers, could not be capable of such calculated violence. As a result, opportunities to intervene were missed, and patterns of poisoning went unrecognized for years. Experts now use her case to teach how societal assumptions can obstruct justice and enable killers to operate under the radar.

In addition, newly declassified court transcripts and interviews have surfaced, offering unprecedented access to her confessions and the methods used by law enforcement. Readers and viewers gain a deeper understanding of her thought process—how she rationalized her actions, the meticulous planning behind each murder, and her chilling ability to maintain an outwardly warm and trustworthy image.

Together, these updates not only reaffirm her place in the annals of true crime but also provide modern audiences with a more nuanced, unsettling perspective: Nannie Doss was not simply a historical figure, but a case study in manipulation, gender bias, and the quiet, hidden dangers that can lurk behind the most familiar faces.

Printed in Dunstable, United Kingdom